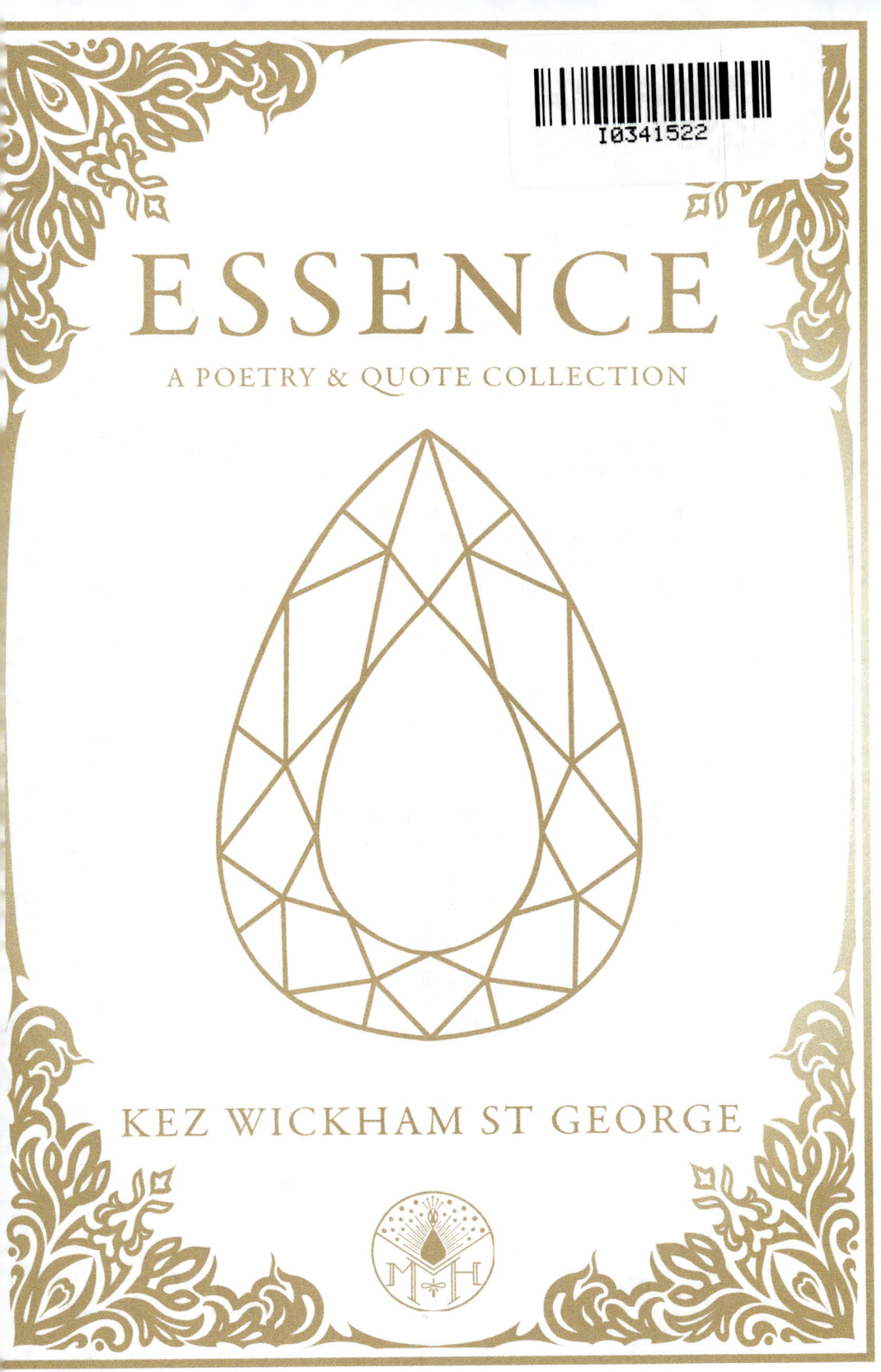

Copyright © Kez Wickham St George

First published in Australia in 2022
by MMH Press
Waikiki, WA 6169

All rights reserved. No part of this book may be used or reproduced by any means, graphic, electronic, or mechanical, including photocopying, recording, taping or by any information storage retrieval system without the written permission of the copyright owner except in the case of brief quotations embodied in critical articles and reviews.

Because of the dynamic nature of the Internet, any web addresses or links contained in this book may have changed since publication and may no longer be vaild. The views expressed in this work are solely those of the author and do not necessarily reflect the views of the publisher and the publisher hereby disclaims any responsibility for them.

Typeset in Adobe Garamond Pro 12/17pt

A catalogue record for this work is available from the National Library of Australia

National Library of Australia Catalogue-in-Publication data:
Essence/Kez Wickham St George

ISBN:
978-0-6454501-0-1
(Hardback)

ISBN:
978-0-6454501-1-8
(Paperback)

ISBN:
978-0-6454501-2-5
(Ebook)

DEDICATION

To my daughter, Demelza
Valued beyond words
Thank you for being you

PROLOGUE

I've always known the power of words; to me, writing was so pleasurable, you could almost taste each word as it dropped onto paper. However, life moved on, to live in Perth WA, where I truly discovered my authorship and my passion for poetry and storytelling.

Then serendipity happened.

I met my publisher, Karen McDermott. Once I became a MMH Press author, 'magic' happened. I was invited to attend a writer's retreat at Crom Castle in Ireland, where I discovered my poetry muse, the words flowed at night as my co-authors slept, words sang in my blood, flowing through my fingers to pen onto paper. I'm a firm believer in synchronicity.

I created this book with the *essence* of joy.

I wish you all enough

Kez

COLOURS OF ME

My heart was heavy its strings sang with grief
family and friends now parted
my questions or how and why not so brief
New friends dried my tears words of wisdom uttered
Relax and look inside of you the answer is there to see

I saw my spirit dance with joy one of love and grace
I watched amazed at its flight and pace
My true colours I now know this is not denied
Oceans of indigo with forests of green
Blue skies that fill the eye
A deep understanding flows in my blood
not the questions of where or why

I emerged from a woman who lay cocoon curled
awakening to my life of beauty
life it is what I make of it
not of others' emotional surging
for I am a woman of many strong passions
now not caring if others don't see
For it's my spirit that now knows the difference
To be true to the Colours of Me

Kez

QUOTE #1

Believe in the magic of your dreams
Live each day completely
The future is your treasure

Adele Basheer

CAST OFF

Cast off they cried
Tears of fear running freely down our faces
Our hearts hammer like metal drums
Our joints of steel rusting in this atmosphere
We came to rescue but we are the hunted
Farewell God speed called our lone friend Sea Dancer
Shadows of pelicans on the white canvas point the way
Tiny bubbles turn into star-studded foam as we head off
Red flying fish cry greetings as they fly over our bow
A raindrop captures the explosion of our planet beneath us
It morphs into the colour of rainbow on spilled oil
Algae bloom still clings to the hull as we lift
To wherever the wind blows us
The faint twitter of land-locked birds fade
As we leave this angry planet
We once called our home.
Kez

QUOTE #2

While we stress about our life and happiness
Life and happiness are happening around us

Kez

WONKY WIRING

my wiring is wonky
I yelled to blue sky,
my on light flickers sadly,
my stop light now fried.

my laugh button is sticky
the tear bucket is full,
eye buttons a tad worn-out,
knee knobs dont pull.

my wires get sticky,
the battery is low,
my guzzle box clicky
brain box goes slow,

my wiring's shonky
my body breaking nonstop,
where do I go to get fixed
why, the wonky wire shop.

Kez

QUOTE #3

To be concerned about what you don't have is
To ignore what you do have

THE GALAHS

They fly cloud-thick with raucous cry
wrenching dreams from sleepy eye.

Pink breasts glowing,
in the rising dawn
they settle on treetops,
they cover dried lawn.

Pecking at grubs,
deep in sandy holes
nibbling berries, jealous chaos unfolds.

Waddling proudly nipping & screeching,
strutting their stuff.
All tells a story,
most of it bluff.

Then lifting as one
back into the sky,
swirling like storm clouds,
their calls echo into a faint sigh.

Kez

QUOTE #4

There are no coincidences in this life
But recognising possibilities of new directions
Then boldly grabbing onto it

DRAWING THE LINE

In the realm of water he was missed far and wide
The silver grandad of all silver fish once puffed with pride
The large, scaled body that would glide with ease
Or hurtle with hunger at the smaller species
They hid in nooks and cranny aplenty
Shivering in fear of silvers tum always empty
His mouth so wide would snap with glee
Munching on shrimp or sand deep pipis
Silver once famous for craft and speed
Cheating death many times
He twisted and turned
Thrashing himself free of line and man's greed
Spitting disdain at bent hook one last time
Soon his turn had come of drawing the line

Kez

QUOTE #5

Obstacles are simply things that frighten you
When you take your eyes off your road

SEA DANCER

My eyes saw what the mind not believed
A fair damsel's form rose from the sea,
Its hand waved in time with the waves flicking by
The sea now dark in tune with night sky,
The red setting sun cast its shadow on wet sand
I stood in wonder to wave back or just stand
Was I the only one who saw this sea dancer
Who danced on dark water
The moon and I her only grandstand
Was I the only one without any answers
Slowly so gently this maiden disappeared
Was I the only one who shed a sad tear

Kez

QUOTE #6

A strong friendship will never die
If it's from the core of the heart

Kez

WEDDING BELLS

Wedding bells ringing,
voices raised & singing,
married bliss to be tested,
single thoughts now arrested.

'Congrats,' 'Good on ya, mate,'
bellowed forth through frothy brew,
backslappers, hand shakers,
line up in a queue.

Rib nudgers, eye winkers,
tired old jokes,
the bride rolls eye to sky,
rude rugby club blokes.

Deep sighs escapes from bridely bra,
'tis cue for groom,
to leave hot smoky bar.

Honeymoon beckons,
a trip so divine,
this time tomorrow,
the Swiss Alpine.

Kez

QUOTE #7

Strength is what we gain
From the need to survive

Kez

DIVIDED IN TWO

Born into a land of mountains and water
Soil of black crumbling loam
Snow-capped peaks piercing cotton-ball clouds
Forest of thick lush green beauty
This is my heart's home.

A land of mist damp muted bounty
Roaring thundering waterfalls
Hot bubbling pools and steaming streams
Boutiques of dainty lacy ferns
Enclosed umbrella of vivid greens.

The country I live in
Stretches mind furrows brow
This huge land of abundance
A time warp of past and now
Your breath is stopped as vastness is viewed
Eye not believing what mind has imbued.

Ghost gums bleached white
Pale green dotted over rocks of burnt red
Burnt tree trunks now spotted with bright green
Promise of life so deep the eye cannot see.

Heat radiates from crevasse and pore
Pools of turquoise shiver with promise
Yellow sand red earth beg for more.

Bruise-coloured sunsets bring deep shadows
Nights vast oval abounds
Huge heavens filled with bright stars
Sunrise to sunset earthly beauty surrounds.

Kez

QUOTE #8

Happiness depends
On the quality of
Your thoughts

K P Weaver

EARTH WIND & FIRE

Fire erupts spitting out its red tongue with cackling glee
Red in its rage indigo and orange
Within its mighty strength

Black earth full of bounty
Virginal mounds of black loam await
To be filled with seed and pods from ruined forests
Winds blow the breath of passion & strength
A race between green treasure or searching beak

Water gurgles gleefully from rivulets and waterfalls
Falling in a rapture of melody a sensuous song
Life once well-hidden begins its journey

To raise its face to bright sun
Earth admiring the beating of new life
Her work for now is done
All elements of life is a mystery

Kez

QUOTE #9

Be careful what and who you tolerate
You're teaching others
How to treat you

Kez

FAITH

Whoever would have thought
one day I would be an elder
my advice trusted heart-centred
not always tactful or tender

Whoever would have thought
what this life has taught me
love can be spliced with logic
no need for the emotional baggage in tow
we the elders have struggled with this and know

How do you tell another
one who thinks they know best
the road you travelled was like no others
that was my life: her life is yet to test

Her journey is her very own
made of laughter love and life with many blunders
her heart seems like it could break in two
my advice is shrugged away
her face scowling like black thunder

You want to hold her oh so close
aching to follow ancient tradition
her angry tears hurting your heart
your words of wisdom she tears apart

Will your words leave an imprint or a shadow
that hopefully one day she too will follow
her premonition like no other
the power of her own recognition

Kez

QUOTE #10

Today you are not
The same person
You were yesterday

Kez

GIRLFRIENDS

Clatter, natter, china clinking
candles inside glass hoods winking
dinner with friends
a bounty of chatter.
Have you heard?
did you see? No! she didn't
questions buzz like busy bees

Bodies talk, jewelled hands aflutter
butterflies would envy this female cluster
minds all saying and thinking alike
quick-witted laughter rattles around
many faces smiling so happy and bright

News of born babies, the male partner cast aside
no tears does she shed, this aging bride
age and body shapes laughed at with glee
what's to discuss? Ooh no it's me.

They rustle and rummage into bags
of all shapes and sizes
memories in colour paraded like prizes
with tears and wobbly grins we hug farewell so tight
promises made of meeting, a future delight
the power of friends so mighty and right

Kez

QUOTE #11

When you seek a life
Of contribution
It also brings in
Personal success

Kez

LILLY

Its roots bound deep within unforgiving mud
Tiny green shoots of life creep into daylight
One lone cone of pale velvet waits
A small white petal unfolds
In its center a golden ray of hope

Kez

QUOTE #12

Real opportunity
For any success
Lies within the person
Not the job

Zig Ziglar

LAST KISS

Tell me you love me
Just say it the once
Let my spirit be opened
To what I pray is just

Tell me you love me
Look into my face
I want to believe you
Your harsh words carry no grace

Please say you love me
For I know not what to do
My heart feels crippled
Inside this boney cage
As I wait for the lawful truth

I see it now an empty void
My plea not heard is lost
Don't hold me back there is no point
Don't yell or make a fuss
The fight is lost our love has gone
To you I don't exist
Hold my hand to say goodbye
Sealed with one last kiss

Kez

QUOTE #13

Some people will never change
Be
Grateful

Kez

MEMORIES

A rush of memory in one small stone
His words of love now encased in a hard portal
His small hand in mine as he bequeathed to me
A promise of undying love
His small voice strong and true

Today he's moved from my side
The stone reminds me every day
Our heartbeats still strong with love
I still feel his hand in mine.

Kez

QUOTE #14

To change your thinking
Change your thinking

Kez

SMILE

A smile of welcome
Our open arms spread wide
I step forward to be embraced
Apart for so long
Loneliness now ambushed
Gone in a blink
Together we stand
United in our friendship

Kez

QUOTE #15

Replace the thought
Why is this happening?
To
What is it trying to teach me?

Kez

MY GIRL

Her chuckle as a babe
Made me smile
It bubbled from deep inside her belly
Then spilled into the room

As a child her delight in everything new
Would stop me to ponder what she saw
I too caught up in the magic
Reflected in her eyes

As a teen her smile faded
Anger flitting in her eyes
A warning of emotions
Her laugh jaded with complex devotions
Who does she love parents or lover more

A woman now stands before me
Her smile is faint
The laughter not reclaimed
For life has taught her many things
To trust another may hurt you in ways yet unknown.

Kez

QUOTE #16

There is always,
always … always
something
to be grateful for.

Kez

PAINTBOX

My paintbox of colours
Many hues in a row
My brush leaves a trail
Droplets of rainbows

My paintbox dazzles
Putting jewellery to shame
With each tinted drop
I see mystic worlds take shape

They shimmer and dance
As my brush gently strokes
Each bright colour calling
The very best from us both

Kez

QUOTE #17

Life is like riding a bike
To keep your balance
Keep moving
But stay on the bike

Julie Randell

MY HAT

If the hat I wear is strickening and thickening
Does it make my mind scrunched up or munched up?
If we swapped hats
How would I feel

Would I be called a fish or an eel
Would I be you or you be me

To wear your hat would I still be me
Or would my face change
A face you could not see

In my hat your face would be wobbly
'Cause my hat's much more knobbly
My hat's been scuffed my hats been bruised
My hat is worn your hat hardly used

I like your hat it suits you good and bold
I like my hat as time has told
So let's not swap but just agree

I can't be you and you can't be me
It's not your hat I choose to wear
My heart not your hat that holds you dear.

Kez

QUOTE #18

It's not about the goal
It's about growing
To become
That person
Who can achieve that goal

Kez

ANGEL IN MY ROOM

A faded painting in my room
of an angel giving prayer
no-one sees her but myself
no-one says a word

At night as I lay with sleep-tired eyes
The house creaking its aged bones
I nestle deep into my bed
Wind and rain beating on windows

There is no fear as I know she's there
A beacon of safety and love
There is angel in my room

Kez

QUOTE #19

Make a promise to yourself
In order to thrive and survive
You will celebrate every day
In some way or other

Kez

WISDOM

In a buoyant sea where I lay
A tiny seed of humanity
Kicking and stretching in this warm brine
A learning of survival ahead of me

Listening to her beating heart, I know it's nearly time
Quietly we have joined soon to be torn apart
Learning so much in this red twilight ocean
Knowledge so wise that this choice was mine

Now pushed into a world of confusing emotions
I soon learn to sit upon knee
Gaining my fill of old-age wisdoms
The words that are spoken
Filled with a musical potion

I learnt on this knee that words can harm
Words can stroke you with love or sadden the heart
Her whispered wisdom leaked deep into my soul
I'm grateful for her love of words
Her wisdom was my gain

Kez

QUOTE #20

No matter the size or shape
Ethnicity or religion
Everyone can change the course
Of their future

Kez

CAMPING

Faces smiling greetings friendly
Away from your workday life
Neither full nor empty

Voices welcoming saying hello
Their frantic lifestyle now on go slow
Green domes rising brown ones to
Little tin boxes on wheels passing through

Tent ropes tight and twangy
Sounds of hammers thwacking pegs
Webs of ropes arise to catch one's legs

People laughing greeting old mates and new
Hi how ya going? How's the world with you?
What did this year bring? Travels near and far
A story is forthcoming it's their turn to star

I sit and listen laugh and sigh
To the tale of a far-off lands
It's proving hard to stay awake
His story very grand

The sun sinks low casting its grand glow
All is quite now as campers go to asleep
I too join those in slumber deep

Kez

QUOTE #21

Be the reason
Someone feels welcome
Valued, loved
And supported

Kez

MY CASE OF MEMORIES

Memories love won and lost
Of friends past and dear with melancholy
Faded photos precious with wear

Tatty torn finger paintings
Strange stick figures all in a line
Mummy and daddy in wriggly letters
To me they're all divine

Trinkets of all sorts abound in this box
Shells, stones, feathers handmade cards
Recollections from many ports

Memories so strong an unbreakable bind
My children's voices calling, 'Look what I've found'
Their baby faces so proud of this important find

My family has grown to some I'm not known
Memories of laughter as we all take our place
Pulling funny faces the camera seals our fate

A life full of riches I'm so glad it's mine
A bounty of memories some good some bad
Tucked aside for another time.

Kez

QUOTE #22

If I'm constantly scratching
At misfortunes
Reacting instead of acting
Mourning the past
Praying for a better future
Instead of living in today
I am missing out
On what the universe is trying to show me

A SCAREDY BEER TALE

Once upon a time there was a village rhyme
That folk from near and far did chant
A song of cheer about the virtues of wine and beer

But some folks from here and there
Whispered these two brews to fear
And so forbid the naughty rhyme
While others brewed a stronger fear

They brewed it in a cauldron huge
It had such a lovely smell
Spice and yeast a dash of green herbs
Claims a sniff or smell would make you well

Now folks heard this silly rhyme
That beer is bad for you
To be on guard was wise
Large letters bold with two crossed bones
Was stuck to either side

Wonder brew now sold in every shop
This brew cleans out tubes and all
Drink this beer it's good for you
Just chug until you pop

There is a lesson for all to tell
This silly rhyme is not a spell
There was a reason it was called
A brew from hell

Kez

QUOTE #23

Is home to your heart just a place to stay
Or is home to your heart a place where
You are loved and love in return?

Kez

HE LOVES ME, HE LOVES ME NOT

He loves me he loves me not
Ring-a-ring o' roses
Rock paper scissors another game
All can make you see
But add no blame

Tissue paper strength unknown
Covers rock of grief and sorrow
Stopping streaming fall of tears
Damning hurt of endless tears

Scissors wait blades set to snap or slice
Cutting cords of beliefs now no strings to tie
Heart do break melt and crumble
Spirit drags with deadly weight
Pray to rock for safety's sake

As you hide inside this place of grace
Your faith in rock a safety place
Scissors poke snip and click

Sharp points will snap when rock shows its power
Paper is its shrouds to cover sparked shower
Don't fret or fear you're safe
Within this rock you can hide

Kez

QUOTE #24

We are made for both joy and woe
When we accept this the better we go

C Dart-Thornton

PHONES

From wall to bench to pocket
It happened in a flash
One day I was winding a handle
All changed with speed
It seemed so fast and brash

Long ago a voice would greet me kindly
She would even know my name
We would spend a while swapping stories
Then back to our chores once again

Years went by the telephone now small
Now sat on bench not attached to wall
It had a dial that whirred once turned
Instant connection with friends insured

Today this phone so small
Is placed in a pocket
A number is tapped no dial in sight
What next, we all wonder
With our human delight.

Kez

QUOTE #25

We all need a lighthouse in our lives
To alert us when danger is ahead
Or to shed a comforting light to find
our way home

Kez

MY CALL

From a distance you will hear my call
The notes rising high
Buffeting edges of scudding clouds
Once released the cascade drops
Raining down into the leafy canopies
Who will listen as they fall

Kez

QUOTE #26

There are no coincidences
In this world
Only recognition of passing possibilities
A new direction
And boldly grabbing hold of it

Kez

TO BE OR NOT TO BE

My name has been forgotten
My body once repelled Neptune's waves
A craft so fine oceans parted before me
Sand now drifts where sea once curled
Joints rust under flotsam of salted years
My demise is near my heart is broken
I silently weep for the love shared between us
My last heart spark leaps with joy
Today the sun floods my wooden ribs
I now hear a whispered invitation
To be embraced within salty depths.

Kez

QUOTE #27

Anything the minds believes and conceives
It will achieve

Kez

NIGHT TIDE

Sliding rolling gliding
A wave of prism colors
Meets the shore
Its passionate boom becomes
A hissing sigh
Its journey now done.

Kez

QUOTE #28

It is the moments of any decision
Your destiny is shaped

A Robbins

TIME

There came a time
When my own light dimmed low
My heartbeat in time
To a pulse slowed with fear

There came a time
When mine eyes saw no beauty
Trapped in a cage of jagged bones
Blood pulsed into deep pools

There came a time
When a voice of light found me
A whisper like a sea of rolling mist
I clung to the bare ribs of my own sinking ship

There came a time
When my own voice became raised in salute
Calling those still in dark places
Cowering in the shades of their own earthy vessels

Kez

QUOTE #29

If you think education is not important
Try living with ignorance

FRIENDSHIP

I would hold you close once more
To say those words I could not before
I would hold you close
Look into your eyes
Explore the sadness
Break down those walls

I would hold you close to simply ask why
Your friendship to me well earnt
Not tied to some device

For friends we are in body and heart
A jigsaw of colors
Dancing patterns of light
I would hold you close
to delay your earthly flight

Kez

QUOTE #30

Sift through sands of offered advice
Finding your own pearl of wisdom

Kez

THOUGHTS

My thoughts drip down
Over my hull of scuttled dreams
Emotions roll like storm-tossed waves
Over razor-sharp reefs
Parted now by my desire
For safe harbour
Connected only
With Neptune's cord

Kez

QUOTE #31

To be concerned over what you don't have
Is a waste of your time
Appreciate what you do have

Kez

INSIDE YOURSELF

Dance to your own tune
March to your own beat
You have more inside you than most
People will begin to know
That now is the time to use
Your own skills and knowledge
To being out just who you are
Create a new path
For you have greatness within you.

Kez

QUOTE #32

Never walk on a well-worn path
It only leads you to where others have been
Create your own

Kez

TIMELESS

Time is slow for those who wait
Fast for those who lament
Short for those that celebrate
But for those of us who love
Time is eternity

William Shakespeare

QUOTE #33

Progress is a step in the right direction
It is not necessarily a step forward

Author Unknown

WHEN

When is it the right time said the caterpillar to the sun
When the time is right the sun warmly replied
Will the wind tell me she asked
The sun beamed its mirth
As the caterpillar stretched and basked

When is the right time she asked the wind
The wind shook with glee saying
It's written in your memory
Will the rain tell me she wanted to know
The rain answered back
Before the snow

They were all correct as time would tell
Her heart said it's time
To weave your cocoon spell
The seasons changed as she slept on

Safely curled from the winters storm
The sun's bright rays woke her winter slumber
Wings of white emerged from
The pod of silken wonder

Kez

QUOTE #34

Follow your heart and your destiny
For this is your life
There is nowhere else to go
Is there?

Kez

MY KNIGHT

For many years
I did wonder
Applauding your shining success
Cringing at my own blunders

I had prayed for such a long time
For this knight in his armour
To whisk me away
Save me from my life's drama

Then one day I realised
I had stepped from frypan to fire
My knight not so bold
His opinion always dire

My life becoming stressful
Every step taken with care
My knight now my jailer
His words a constant fear

His love for me no longer
He had not been what he seemed
I wonder where the magic went
Or if it was all a dream

Kez

QUOTE #35

Love is the best medicine
In the score of life
Without it one would forever be
Out of tune
In the immense choir of humanity

COUNTRY GIRL

Scuffed jean, faded jeans ponytail hair
Bronzed skin brown eyes
Freckles spread across cheeks
Laughter readily spills
Generous smiles shared

Kez

QUOTE #36

Empowerment is the sweet nectar
From bushland that had blossomed
After chaos has ravaged our earth

Kez

MY ARMCHAIR

It sits like a waiting servant
Waiting for me its owner
To heave a heavy sigh
As my body lowers its limbs
Into the cushiony depths

Kez

QUOTE #37

Why repeat the old errors
If there are many to complete

WHAT IF

What if our religion was each other?
If our practice was our life?
If prayer were our everyday words?
What if the temple was the earth?

If the forests were our churches?
If holy water was the lakes rivers and oceans?
And what if meditation was our relationship?

If the teacher was life?
If wisdom was self-knowledge ?
And if love was the center of our being?

Author Unknown

QUOTE #38

Many of us lose the small joys
Of life
Looking for their happiness

SUNFLOWER

Wind gently nudges
Tall elegant stems
Like bright lights
Their open faces sway
Each seeking the light

Kez

QUOTE #39

There are people who speak to us but do not listen.
There are people who will hurt us deeply but leave no scar.
Then there are those people who simply appear in our lives
and will place a mark on it forever

TOGETHER

The power of these times
Lies in the rise of our equal leadership
Standing together to find
Balance and solutions to the earth's problems.

President J F Kennedy

QUOTE #40

Take what is good from your past
&
Build your future from it

Kez

PEARL

Wet hard barnacle-encrusted shell
Clamped tightly over bounty
Inherited fear from birth

Jaw of muscle clamped open
Invasion of womb like meat
Shuddering aching surrender
Of bounty ocean deep

Birth from virginal hiding
Illustrious perfect orb residing
Mother of fortune cast aside
Globe of fame and fortune rising

Kez

QUOTE #41

What you go through
Will help you get through

Adele

STAND TALL

There were times
When I wanted to yell
From the highest of mountains
I'm have a voice listen to me

There were times
When I wanted the rich & famous
To enfold me in their dreams
To be one with them

Now as I look back
Power of the ancients
Sings through my veins
No longer do I seek approval

Kez

QUOTE #42

A person without a goal
Is like ship without a rudder

Kez

ENERGY

If you intend your life with passion
Create a vision not a mission
Why weary the body with toil
When the mind will till the fertile soil

Breathe in the air of mountain or ocean
Blood flowing freely to energise motion
Feel the deep thud of a grateful heart
Embrace your life force from the very start

Kez

QUOTE #43

We are all self-made
However
Only the few will admit it

Nightingale

XMAS WISH

How I loved to hold
Their small hands in mine
To stare at the night sky
With each scudding cloud
We would see Santa's sleigh

As years went by
Growth from child to adult
We still gathered on Xmas eve
Tradition in its place

My heart ached to hear
The magic of childish awe
When a hand slipped into mine
A whispered voice claiming
I see reindeer dancing in a line

Kez

QUOTE #44

We can think *Those were the days*
Or think *I'm living my dream*

Kez

CHOCOLATE EGGS

In a basket made of straw
Covered in pretty tinsel paper
Six small eggs lay

Each one tempting me to take one bite
To satisfy the craving of sugar
I knew my tastebuds would receive

To walk away would be a shame
My hand shakes as it reaches for one
Knowing in an hour there would be none.

Kez

QUOTE #45

Don't compromise yourself
You're all you've got

SILVER FISH

In a clear pond of aqua blue
Made by the distant ocean
The tide had swept clean
The shoreline dotted with seabirds

Each black beady eye
Waiting for me to leave
Their silver prey swimming innocently
I was their guardian
A duty I had not asked for

I hunch over them knowing
Certain death was blowing
In the Indian ocean wind

Kez

QUOTE #46

Even the best of us
Sometimes eat their words

TIME OUT

Time is all we have
We are clocked in at birth
The clock stops as does destiny

Kez

QUOTE #47

Each of us create our universe around us
When we should be creating it within us

Kez

RETURN

If I could return to the places I once knew
And meet those folks that I once called mine
I would take that chance and greet them
Just to sit with them and listen
Once more to the tales of what was

I would tell them my story

As now I can add
That my life was very different
Sometimes happy sometimes sad

If I could meet them one more time
To sit and listen to their stories not mine
I would take great pleasure in adding my story
My words cascading then blending
Into the lines of our past history

To lay my head down in its need to rest
To close my eyes no need to fear
For I'm now with those that I held dear

Kez